TEXAS is...

the Sesquicentennial Remembered

To: The Raschke's

TEXAS is. . .

the Sesquicentennial Remembered, *and wonderful people like you.*

By
Mark Holbrook

October, 1986

Published By

 **Ringtail PRODUCTIONS LIMITED**

A
LIMITED EDITION
NUMBER
365/1000

TEXAS is...

Layout and design: E. W. Rock

Photographs: Barry Snidow, Jim Picquet, E. W. Rock, Mark Holbrook and Bob Amdall

Printed by Taylor Publishing Company, Dallas, Texas.

Copies of this book may be purchased by contacting the publisher: Ringtail Productions Limited, P.O. Box 161084, Irving, Texas, 75016.

ISBN 0-9617487-0-2

A Limited Edition printing, October, 1986

ACKNOWLEDGEMENTS

An idea stands little chance of reaching maturity if it is conceived in isolation and reared without the benefits of a nurturing family. I was fortunate to have a wonderful surrogate family assisting in this endeavor.

Jim Widener: who initially encouraged me by providing a forum for my early writings;

Bev Flusche: a gracious Cajun lady whose proofreading skills would match those of an Oxford scholar;

Keith Marks: an attorney whose counsel, wisdom and friendship far exceeded any fees paid;

Barry Snidow: a bright, emerging photographer whose pictures are bold, striking and sensitive;

Jim Picquet: a friend and associate whose Texana photography is both a living passion and an art form;

E. W. Rock: the publisher of *The Journal* whose personal and professional touch in the layout design of this book gave each page a singular identity;

Helen Lance: who made the first time experience of working with a quality major book printer an enlightening and educational process;

Dorothy and Earl Wells: owners of Commercial Printing who gave new meaning to the term "rush order" when accommodating my collateral printing needs;

Irma Janicek: owner of Artist's Corner Studio whose design talents captured the spirit and heritage of Texas on the brochure;

Gerald Stavely: a supportive friend, businessman and native of Tennessee who would have been there like the Tennessee patriots of 1836 had it been necessary.

Finally, to each respondent who took the time to share their own personal thoughts, perspectives and humor regarding this grand state, "You done good!"

Mark Holbrook
Irving, Texas

For Patrick and Jennifer who now realize that adults dream too, and Judy who believed in the dream.

7

TEXAS is

150 years old this year and by most standards, still an infant of the world community; taking a whole year off to celebrate in a style expected, perhaps even demanded, of a state whose stature is recognized world-wide; remembering the past, by the people of the present for the generations to come who will judge the accomplishments and significance of this legacy when celebrating the bicentennial in the year 2036; 265,000 square miles of contrasting and diverse peoples, places and geography; the memories, heritage, images — both past and present — and events that are sometimes grand and often times insignificant which make this state truly unique; the historic year of the Sesquicentennial remembered

This year marks the 150th anniversary of Texas independence. It is also the 100th anniversary of the Texas State Fair and the 50th anniversary of the opening of the great Hall of State.

But whether we're celebrating 150 years, 100 years or just 50, we're still celebrating a quality that's manifested in the heart of Texas and that has endured throughout Texas' history. It's the Texas spirit and the Texas pride.

As we celebrate the Sesquicentennial, let us reaffirm the principles embodied in Texas: independence, courage and freedom.

Happy birthday, Texas.

George Bush

OFFICE OF THE GOVERNOR
STATE CAPITOL
AUSTIN, TEXAS 78711

MARK WHITE
GOVERNOR

   "In this Sesquicentennial year, one is constantly reminded of
the effect Texas has had on the world. When one thinks of heroes of
struggles for independence, doesn't the Alamo come to mind? And when
one thinks of music and literature, there is a staggering list of native sons and daughters who rank among the world's top performers,
composers, and authors. What about the affect of Texas politicians
on the nation?   One can't forget President Lyndon Johnson or House
Speaker Sam Rayburn. When one mentions Texas to someone from out of
the state, images spring quickly to mind: the Lone Star, oilwells,
chili, and cowboy hats and boots. One thing is certain. Texas and
Texans will continue to make their mark on the nation and world."

                                        Mark White
                                        Governor of Texas

. . .: explaining the nutritional value of fried okra and black-eyed peas to a visiting northern house guest; a two-fisted bar-b-q sandwich with an icy mug of Pearl beer from Sonny Bryan's in Dallas . . .

"One of the ancient Roman poets, Horace, wrote a poem about a country whose civilization had collapsed. 'They had no poet and they died,' he wrote. Texas has been blessed with many native sons who wrote about its ample geography, its wildlife, its cowboys, and all of the things that make up the mystique and grandeur that is Texas. They have left a rich legacy in song and saga, celebrating the heroes that have always been larger than life — Bigfoot Wallace, Sam Houston, Davy Crockett, Cactus Jack Garner; and the landmarks, such as the Alamo, the Big Bend country, the Texas Navy, the Chicken Ranch. As long as the poets thrive, Texas will remain a vigorous, productive state. In the words of a popular song, 'We've only just begun'."

JOHN D. VAUGHAN
President
Poetry Society of Texas

. . .. a young child's joy in finding a genuine sand dollar while combing the beaches of Padre Island; a young Mexican dripping from the muddy water of the Rio Grande while running through the brush of the border chasing the dream of all those who have beaten a path and made the run before him

"With 1985 Dr Pepper's Centennial year, and 1986 the Sesquicentennial year for Texas, it is timely and fitting to acknowledge the two anniversaries since both seek to preserve the rich legacy of a comparable period in American history.

Texas and Dr Pepper encountered many common problems and opportunities in their pioneer days which history reveals were accounted for in a creditable manner.
Texas and its people turned vast undeveloped resources into great opportunities which were expanded far beyond its borders. Dr Pepper and its people, likewise, capitalized on opportunities to spread its operations well beyond Texas and into many parts of the world.

Dr Pepper has long been proud of its heritage as a "Native Texan" and salutes Texas on its Sesquicentennial anniversary."

W. W. CLEMENTS
Chairman
Dr Pepper Company

... memories of a native son lying in a muddy rice field in Viet Nam wondering if the folks back home really understand; a Sunday lunch of Southern fried chicken, mashed potatoes, corn-on-the-cob and vine ripened tomatoes washed down with cold milk poured from a cobalt blue pitcher at a favorite aunt's home in Rosebud ...

"Hawaii recalls with pride the 1944 rescue of the 'Lost Battalion' of the 141st Texas Infantry Regiment by Hawaii's own 442nd Regimental Combat Team during heavy fighting in France in World War II. This action and related cooperation between Texans and Hawaii's Americans of Japanese ancestry in the European Theater forged a strong bond of friendship and esteem between our states. Hawaii's Army unit was awarded the Presidential Unit Citation for its heroism during that historic engagement."

GEORGE R. ARIYOSHI
Governor
State of Hawaii

18

19

Tom Landry

"I am proud of the great heritage that the State of Texas has that goes all the way back to the Alamo. Texans have a special place in their hearts for this Giant state, its beautiful and varied landscape, its down-to-earth and friendly residents and for the Lone Star which symbolizes our overwhelming pride in Texas -- the land that we love. "

Tom Landry

COWBOYS CENTER ★ ONE COWBOYS PARKWAY ★ IRVING, TEXAS 75063-4727

...patches of Bluebonnets and Indian paint brush dotting the roadway shoulders of Interstate Highway 35 near Round Rock; an icy Lone Star longneck while waiting in line at Joe T. Garcia's Mexican restaurant in Fort Worth...

"Years ago my good friend, Judge Julien Hyer, of the 44th District Court, wrote a book about the Brazos River country that he named *The Land of Beginning Again.*

Later I rather resented Judge Hyer's use of that title, for I would have put it on one of my books. Texas is the place a man moved after running out of money and luck and — perhaps — health. He scratched 'G.T.T.' across his door, nailed it shut, and headed for Texas.

Texas offered hope for the millions who came. It was a place for a new start — a land of beginning again — for my people, 141 years ago, as it is for those who come now."

JUNE R. WELCH
Author and Historian

... a blood-red sunset fading over the Davis Mountains; peering through a glass bottom boat at Aquarina Springs and realizing as the aquifer bubbles forth there can be no measuring of time when infinity is a variable

"This is a proud year for Texas as I think of its size, natural beauty and cultural heritage. We are a state populated by a diversified people who are proud of their heritage, work hard day-to-day, and look forward to future opportunities.

Yet years ago, what it meant to be a Texan was to do the best one could with whatever one had. This was true when Texas undertook the challenge to tame the frontier, whether it was to herd the cattle, make the crops bloom or sink a wildcat oil well.

If times are tough for Texans, that is nothing new. Our state was born in the midst of a struggle, a struggle to survive the fearful days between the Alamo and San Jacinto. Always Texans have come through, because that is the sort of people we are — stubborn, courageous and free.

Texas is a land of opportunity and individual achievement. It reflects every aspect of the American way of life and the American dream.

As we commemorate our Sesquicentennial, let us salute the special people who make it a very special part of America."

PHIL GRAMM
United States Senator, Texas

. . . a varied terrain and climate that was kissed by God at creation, but later subleased to the Devil each August; riding the mechanical bull at Gilley's in Pasadena . . .

"The fact that I am a native Texan from Weatherford has given me added strength and courage to tackle an almost impossible task!

I have decided to constantly try to reach my ultimate and evangelical goal of teaching these foreigners from other states and countries how to speak the true and pure language of Texas. This task is one that could only be accomplished by a native Texan.

I hope that all native Texans everywhere will join me in my campaign during this grand and glorious sesquicentennial year. With a task as tough as this one . . . I need all the help I can get!"

SHARON BEAUCHAMP
Publication Consultant

28

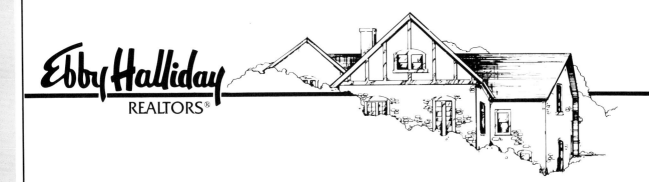

REALTORS®

The difference between a fairy tale and a Texas tale is:

A fairy tale begins "Once upon a time", whereas a Texas tale begins"Now you sonsaguns won't believe this"!

Well, when my company transferred me in 1938 from the small town in the midwest to the great state of Texas, it was like a fairy tale.

And when I saw the opportunities Texas presented for the entrepreneur, I wrote back to friends, "Now you sonsaguns won't believe this!"

It has been just that wonderful!

Ebby Halliday

Ebby Halliday, REALTOR

... dancing the Cotton-Eyed Joe at Billy Bob's Texas in Fort Worth; a close election in Duvall County with 110% of the population voting ...

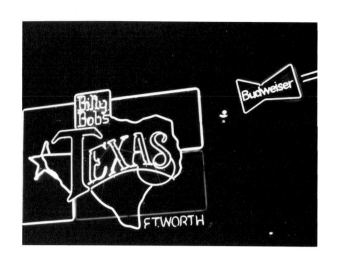

"Texas, more than any other state it seems, goes far beyond the common perceptions held by most people — it is cowboys and computer chips; it is oil wells and oceanography."

MARVIN TATE
Mayor
City of Bryan

"A true Texan is a person who ever wonders why Texas ever joined the union."

LYNN S. WYATT
Houston Civic Leader

. . . a Vietnamese family struggling to learn and understand a foreign culture and language necessary for survival in Sabine Pass; the brow-sweating, nose-running sensation of a "bowl of red" from Tolbert's Texas Chili Parlor in Dallas

"Education has become the turbocharger to push people ahead in a competitive society which bases promotion on performance and merit. So everybody wants some of it. In the past when people lost their jobs, they waited, or moved on, or took a more menial position. Today college enrollments go up every time unemployment rates go up.

Texas in 1986 is at a crossroads in higher education. In economic terms the state has just entered the post-industrial society. That is, we are increasingly mnore dependent on knowledge, information, services, creative ideas, and quick transfer of technology than in the past. Even the pre-industrial and in-dustrial enterprises which continue to serve as a major support for our economy now draw on the knowledge base and employs the graduates produced by our colleges and universities. We must substitute expertise in the knowledge and information fields for the raw energy our ancestors put into taming and developing the rough frontier that has rewarded us so richly until now."

KENNETH H. ASHWORTH
Texas Commissioner of Higher Education

... wanting to stay in the depths of Wonder World Cave until the July heat fades to October coolness; finding missing collectibles at the Traders Village "Texas Flea Market" in Grand Prairie

"Well, I feel like a Texan. I'm 68 and if youth is this good I can hardly wait for middle age!"

MICKEY SPILLANE
Writer

"Ah, the Texas Press; some mayors in Texas have a problem with them, not me! You see, 'they print the truth and I deny it'!"

MALCOLM CLARK
Mayor
City of Port Arthur

"Texas is pride in your country, your state, your community, your family. My cousin and I were so proud of our family that we hired a fellow to do our family tree — we paid him to look it up and had to pay him twice as much to keep it quiet."

ROLAND A. TEAL
Rancher
Oakwood

Ninfa R. Laurenzo
Chairman of the Board

"The mixing of the two cultures of Texas and Mexico has brought about one of the great cuisines of the world in Texas. There is no finer eating anywhere than Tex-Mex Mexican food, cooked with the love and care by the people of Mexican-American heritage who have made Texas their home."

Ninfa Laurenzo

Ninfa Laurenzo

Geosource Plaza • 2700 Post Oak Blvd., Suite 1550 • Houston, Texas 77056

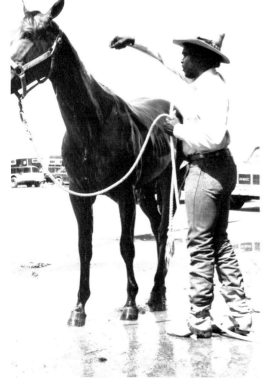

. . .: the bay of hounds treeing a coon on a clear, cool evening in the woods near Kountze; wondering what the elderly gentleman's other source of income might be as he wanders along the expressway picking up aluminum cans near Austin .

"Blanco is a German descent area where tradition thrives, the German language can be understood, and heritage is part of everyday life. Sweet rice, homemade noodles, venison sausage and some old ways of doing things are the common here. The biggest local ongoing social and recreational event is NINE pin bowling. Some two hundred locals gather at the Blanco Bowling Club and Restaurant to drink beer and bowl on alleys that are still set by hand. The alleys are the only part that resembles regular 10 pin bowling. Each week night there is a lot of noise near the center of town.

There is no way to change my pride for being a part of Blanco or Texas. Our forefathers got us where we are today. Let us hope and pray that our descendants have pride in the way we conducted ourselves."

MARGE WAXLER
Mayor
City of Blanco

bureaucrats deploring the tightness of budgets while conversing over mobile cellular phones in vehicles also provided at taxpayers' expense; walking the battlefield of San Jacinto and returning to the present with a feast at the San Jacinto Inn

"Texas — so big, so great, so considerate — to be one of the only places left in the world where it is legal to drive with a cold beer in the open. That is the preservation of positive legislation."

DAN AYKROYD
Comedian, Writer and Actor

"As Governor of the Sooner State, there has always been a warm spot in my heart for Baja Oklahoma."

GEORGE NIGH
Governor
State of Oklahoma

41

wondering if Cut and Shoot will ever produce another heavyweight contender the likes of Roy Harris; explaining to visitors that Southfork Ranch is a tourist front for images grossly exaggerated

"On March 1, 1836, a group of Texans met at Washington on the Brazos to discuss the fate of Texas. Collin McKinney was one of those men. He helped draft the Texas Declaration of Independence and subsequently signed the document on March 2, 1836.

About twelve years later State Representative Collin McKinney introduced legislation that required the county seat of several counties to be within one mile of the geographic center of the county. Thus moving the county seat of Collin County from Buckner to what ultimately became McKinney.

After the Civil War a McKinney pioneer, James Webb Throckmorton, was elected Governor of Texas. Governor Throckmorton had also served as a General in the Confederate Army. Consequently, the Carpetbaggers (or Reconstructionists) did not approve of the way he ran his office, and had him removed after serving one year of a two year term.

During the past 150 years of Texas history, McKinney has provided many good leaders in state and federal government. It is this heritage and legacy that elevates present elected officials and gives us courage to achieve above our normal capacity."

JIM LEDBETTER
Mayor
City of McKinney

State of Tennessee

LAMAR ALEXANDER GOVERNOR

Tennesseans are prouder of Texans that anyone except Texans because so many Texans have Tennessee grandparents.

For a while in the early 1800's, it seemed like Tennesseans went to Texas than stayed at home. GTT -- Gone to Texas -- was carved into log cabins all over our mountains. Davy Crockett, Jim Bowie, Sam Houston, 33 of the men who died at the Alamo -- all came from Tennessee. That's why today Texans and Tennesseans are the only Americans without an accent! So many Texans have Tennessee grandparents. And that's why, outside of Texas, Tennesseans are the biggest celebrators of the Texas Sesquicentenniel.

Lamar Alexander

Governor of Tennessee

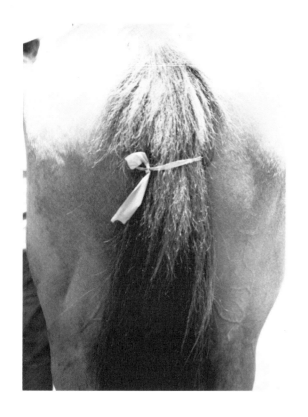

. . .: the smell of burning flesh and hair as new stock are branded on a ranch near Kingsville; a cold fall evening watching the Odessa High School football team play in the tradition born of oil field roughnecks

"There's always been a good deal of confusion in eastern minds about the size and borders of our state. Most out-of-towners can't quite place the borders accurately — particularly our southern flank.

When I was a young Member of the U.S. House of Representatives in the mid 1960s, I recall that a fellow Member who represented a Northeastern state (I am compelled to hold the name of the Member and the state a secret — out of courtesy, you know) approached me one day and said, 'Well, sir, I must say you speak extraordinarily good English.' And the remark, good-natured as it was, had that ring of surprise as if to say, 'I really can't believe you speak English!'

So I smiled broadly at my new friend and said, 'Thank you for the compliment — but my family has lived north of the Rio Grande since 1710, and I imagine that's before your family left Ireland!'

We've been fine friends ever since!"

E. (Kika) de la GARZA
United States Congressman, Texas

the broken silence of dawn as a mockingbird begins a medley of songs; realizing that your One Hour Martinizing will be ready long before the opportunity exists to exit Central Expressway in Dallas on a Friday afternoon

"There is no 'antidote' for the Texas experience. Once you have been 'exposed,' you get this taste for chili every spring, break out in a rash at the prospect of a party — and the loss of your Neiman-Marcus charge takes away your will to live."

ERMA BOMBECK
Author and Columnist

"The true mystique and strength of Texans is their perpetual independence. When others hesitate, they move forward. When things get tough, Texans get tougher. This spirit was born out of the prairies and open spaces that are a part of the Texas tradition. They fought for independence and now they use it to the consternation of many of the rest of the States."

N. ALEX BICKLEY
Dallas Civic Leader

"The sun has riz, the sun has set, but here we is, in Texas yet. Ever' durn thing in this State will bite or poison or stick or sting a feller."

JIMMIE R. PICQUET
Director
John E. Connor Museum

... the sun rising over the Gulf of Mexico on Galveston beach signaling the end of an all night high school prom celebration and the dawn of a new age of responsibility; sampling sofkey in the dining room at the Alabama-Coushatta reservation near Woodville ...

"Texas is... well... Texas IS. Texas cannot be boxed, gift wrapped, microwaved, or dehydrated. Texas was, is, and will be, too big and too diverse for all the invaders from Paleo-Americans to Spaniards to Anglos to Michiganers to completely change. Like the face of the moon its NASA-based astronauts visited, it is pitted from the impact of numberless hordes. All have changed Texas, altered it, left some mark on their passing. But Texas survives, it endures, and if it never quite achieves its potential, because of self-denial more than anything else, Texas always IS." (1)

ARCHIE P. McDONALD
Executive Director
East Texas Historical Society

. . .: realizing that a tour guide in the state capitol has an uncommon command of Texas history, facts and events; memories of Saturday night dances, cheap beer and bloody shirts in Snook . . . .

"The State of Texas influences the world culture through the contributions many of her own have made to cultural and educational progress."

DALE PARNELL
President
American Association of Community and Junior Colleges

...time travel back to the age of dinosaurs in Glen Rose and wondering why some of the tracks point towards Washington; fresh warm boudin and a loaf of French bread from Nick's Grocery Store in Port Arthur

"A short Texas tale:

There was this good ol boy, a traveling man, he was going through deep East Texas when he ran over a coon dog. A fine one, big black and tan. Being a dog lover himself, and a decent fellow, he went up to the farm house and knocked on the door and sadly related his story to the farmer's wife.

She shook her head sadly, told the traveling man how much her husband loved that dog, and said, 'You better go tell him yourself. He's out back in the barn. And listen, make it easy on him. At first, tell him it was one of the kids'."

GORDON BAXTER
Writer and Columnist

. .·. ... a college freshman learning the fine art of dusting a shuffleboard table in a Beaumont bar and wondering if life really becomes any more difficult than this; the devil-may-care attitude of rodeo riders at the Texas Prisoners' Rodeo in Huntsville

"As the old saying a rose is a rose is a rose: a Texan is a Texan is a Texan as the whole world has their eyes on Texas."

GENE DOUGET
Mayor
City of Cut and Shoot

"I was born in Weatherford, Parker County, Texas beside the largest pecan tree in this great state. Ever since that very advantageous beginning, I have felt that this is the grandest state in the U.S.

We, as Texans, have many opportunities, and I believe that some of the greatest things in life are in store for us."

LEE YOUNG
Banker and Civic Leader
Weatherford

*. . . feeling the chill of flesh bumps as the Fightin'
Texas Aggie Band marches across the turf of Kyle
Field at halftime; an aging politician growing much
older and wiser with the former progressing at a much
faster rate than the latter*

"The State of Texas will always have a special
meaning for me because it is where my father,
Conrad N. Hilton, launched a company which
spread itself around the world. It has special
meaning because Texas is my birthplace.

I believe that we Texans are not born; we're
branded with a Lone Star spirit which remains
with us throughout our lives. And wherever the
Hilton flag flies around the globe, you can bet
your Stetson that same spirit is flying high
alongside."

BARRON HILTON

Chairman
Hilton Hotels Corporation

Considering Texas is the land of
abundance, it's people are lean.
It's cities are so cosmopolitan it is
easier to recognize a texan in New York
than it is in the state of Texas.

Texas women have a mind of their own,
so nobody owns them...no problem, Texas
men all do their thing.

The result is when you visit Texas you
feel comfortable because they just
want you to be yourself as they do.
It's just plain "Welcome Stranger".

LeRoy Neiman, New York City

LEROY NEIMAN

watching the muddy waves crash against the granite breakwaters as ships slide through the Intercoastal canal near Groves; staring at cloud formations while floating down the San Marcos river on an old tractor tire innertube

"Too many people have a simplistic image of Texas. To them Texas is the cowboy, sitting tall on a horse in the middle of a desert, or the legendary oilman wielding his power in a steel-and-glass tower twenty stories up. But Texas is diversity. Amarillo is not like Brownsville. El Paso is not like Texarkana, or Houston like Fort Worth. Texas is probably the greatest melting pot in the country aside from the East Coast, an ethnic mixture not only of the Anglo-Saxon heritage but of Black, Mexican, German, French, Swedish, Polish and so many others, including in recent times a considerable sprinkling of Orientals, seeking freedom from today's brand of tyranny, as so many found freedom here from tyrannies of the past. We have so little in common, yet we have so much, for whatever else we or our forebearers may have been, we are all Texans."

ELMER KELTON
Author

the fall season when individuals who are generally normal in appearance and behavior turn into Horned Frogs, Owls, Cougars, Longhorns, Mustangs, Red Raiders, Bears and Aggies; viewing the tradition of Texas' past at the Texas Ranger Museum in Waco

"I am proud to be a native TEXAN and have traveled to many parts of the world. To me, and our family, TEXAS is a model state. It's great in every respect and we are among the 'privileged ones' to live here and enjoy the good life in TEXAS."

JACK W. EVANS
President, Cullum Companies
Former Mayor, City of Dallas

"Texans, more than most Americans, fear being just average, which is fine because Texans aren't average — they are above average, way above average."

BOB BULLOCK
Comptroller of Public Accounts
State of Texas

THE POSTMASTER GENERAL
Washington, DC 20260-0010

Not long ago, a popular television commercial boasted that Texas is so big it can be Monday at one end of the state and Saturday at the other. This <u>slight</u> exaggeration aside, suffice it to say that <u>our</u> great state is large enough in scope and history to have blended more than two dozen racial and ethnic cultures into a single experience that is, at once, completely American and uniquely Texan. Wherever you walk in Texas, you walk among free men and women of proud heritage. I am proud to call Dallas my home!

Albert V. Casey

...driving down a dusty dirt road in East Texas which leads to a faded white clapboard church where twenty-seven Black voices sing a song of praise that transcends all earthly bounds; riding bareback at full gallop through an open pasture and then jumping into the Celina gravel pits for a quick skinny dip

"The spirit and mystique of Texas is known worldwide. While traveling outside the state and in almost any foreign country, a Texan proudly acknowledges his privilege of living in a special part of the United States. The great heritage and reputation for pioneering, independence, and personal freedom sets this state apart from all others. I am proud to be a Texan."

DENTON A. COOLEY, M.D.
Surgeon-in-Chief
Texas Heart Institute

"Good Cajuns never die, they just move to Texas and think they have gone to heaven."

A. J. JUDICE
Crawfish Racing Commissioner
Bridge City

finding and removing ticks after a weekend campaign trip to Possum Kingdom Lake; feeling a lump in your throat as the crowd sings "The Eyes of Texas" in Memorial Stadium on a crisp and clear November afternoon

"Campaigning with these tough and rugged individuals of the Lone Star State was a tremendous experience for me. You find these people to be intelligent, friendly, cheerful, helpful and cordial. They are genuinely interested, with praise, and considerate of others. Add to this a good sense of humor, loads of patience, a dash of humility and you will know a real Texan."

PRESTON SMITH
Former Governor
State of Texas

"The history of Texas and its founders and early settlers have set an example for us of hard work, perseverance and courage to face the future. Can we do less than try to follow their example so that future Texans can enjoy the beauties and joys that we have known?"

EMMETT F. LOWRY
Mayor
City of Texas City

...a foreign land developer planning a future development with little regard, or concern for the heritage that pioneered this proud land before him; the beauty of the massively sculptured Mustangs of Las Colinas in Irving

"Mayoring in Texas; some days, I'd rather garden than govern — at least then I can call a spade a spade. It's been tough being on the council. Too many decisions are bread and butter ones and I'm a pie in the sky person. It's time I stopped being the parade and started spectatoring again."

BARBARA TIEKEN
Mayor
City of New Braunfels

"To paraphrase that great Texan and patriot, Sam Houston, Texans have always known that a great destiny awaited them. This conviction has become part of the American tradition. We will always be indebted to Texas for its robust confidence in American values, and its pride in our contribution to western civilization."

GENERAL ALEXANDER HAIG (Retired)
Former Secretary of State

Hank Snow

POST OFFICE BOX 1084
NASHVILLE, TENNESSEE 37202

WSM GRAND OLE OPRY
AND TV

I was born in Eastern Canada and was an entertainer touring
Canada and recording for RCA Victor Records from 1936 to
1942. During these years, I worked various theater circuits,
doing a 20-minute gig between shows. Every chance I got
during the western features, my eyes and heart focused on
the Lone Star State of Texas. In fact, I have written
various songs about Texas such as THE GALVESTON ROSE; MY
SWEET TEXAS BLUE BONNET QUEEN and others. I finally made
it to Texas in 1949, when I moved from the West Coast to
Dallas. Here I was to get my big break, and you guessed it -
it came from a true blue Texan who turned out to become my
best friend in country music - The Late Ernest Tubb, The Texas
Troubadour. He placed me on the world famous Grand Ole Opry,
after battling with the big wheels who ran the Opry; and on
January 7, 1950, I joined the Opry and I am now in my 37th
year. Thanks to the beautiful State of Texas for raising a
great Texan who made it possible for my family and me to
share the American Dream.

HANK SNOW

... the erratic flight patterns of sea gulls following shrimp boats on their return to Aransas Pass; fresh hot peach and apple kolaches from a bakery in West

"I firmly believe that Texas and Texans have a heritage second to none in our work ethic as well as a personal kinship with our fellow Texans. There still prevails a pioneer spirit in Texas that limits our acomplishments only to that which we limit ourselves."

C. SCOTT PARKER
Mayor
City of Liberty

"Having come to this great state so often to give my seminars, I have come to regard Texas as my second home. However, some of you folks may not take too kindly to that if you saw my first home."

DANNY SIMON
Television Comedy Writer

... a foggy morning in the mosquito teeming swamps and rice fields near Port Acres awaiting migrating geese; a high school youth deciding on a career in aerospace after visiting the LBJ Space Center in Houston ...

"Having lived the latter half of Texas' 150 years, I become more appreciative every day of our Texas heritage and the wonderful opportunities we have enjoyed as citizens of this great State. Texas has had more historic moments than any other State, and I like the way we have preserved and are preserving the Texas heritage. Let's hope there will be cause for as much pride and appreciation when future Texans celebrate our Bicentennial in 2036 A.D."

PRICE DANIEL
Former Governor
State of Texas

... watching a bullfight in Juarez and realizing that the crowd's emotions are the same as a Sunday afternoon professional football game; experiencing the danger and beauty of a river raft ride in Big Bend Park

"One of our 42 distributors in Texas recently sold his 100-millionth case of Coors beer. If that many cases were laid end to end, they would stretch the width of Texas more than 30 times. That's a sizeable record even for Texas! So, congratulations on your Sesquicentennial and, to all of you, a BIG thank you from Coors."

W. K. COORS
Chairman
Adolph Coors Company

THE SECRETARY OF THE INTERIOR
WASHINGTON

Texas is both a place and an attitude. It is a place so large and diverse that I couldn't describe it to anyone without damage to my reputation as an honest and straight-forward person. But I can describe the Texas attitude. It is the belief that you can do about anything you put your mind to and that with brains, muscle, tenacity and a healthy dose of exuberance, great things are accomplished. The State of Texas is a monument to that attitude, which has spilled over on the rest of America and helped make this a better country. Thanks, Texas.

DONALD PAUL HODEL

participating in a rattlesnake round-up and cook-off in Sweetwater; observing foreign corporate visitors dressed in new Levi jeans and starched shirts pretending to be riders of the old west on a dude ranch near Flower Mound

"A Texas friend once said to me: 'Don't ever buy anything that eats.' Pretty interesting advice from someone in the cattle business."

JOHN GAVIN
Ambassador to Mexico

"Recognition of our past through present Sesquicentennial celebrations, combine to seal our future heritage."

GEORGE W. MARTI
Mayor
City of Cleburne

... a remembrance of earlier pioneers' efforts by a contemporary group of hardy, courageous and dedicated modern wagoneers whose spirit of adventure and belief in the preservation of the past traveled over 3,000 miles, visited hundreds of cities and relived a portion of the Texas heritage with a six-month odyssey in wagons drawn by horses and mules known as The Texas Wagon Train

memories of all the wagon train participants who made the trek from Sulphur Springs to Fort Worth the long way and branded a new spirit of pride and heritage in the thousands of individuals who turned out to greet and wish them well

... a sense of patience for an elderly gentleman driving 45 mph on the Gulf Freeway during rush hour traffic; Denton's pride in being the only city that has produced two reigning Miss Americas ...

"Anyone who has lived in west Texas knows the curious three dimensional quality of the landscape. Looking at the Franklin Mountains in El Paso or the Permian reef at Guadalupe Peak is like looking through a child's viewfinder; you have the sense of being able to reach behind the mountains to the spaces you see there.

There is a correspondense between this great clarity of vision and the attitudes of west Texans. There is no room for subterfuge. Everything is direct and clear, like the air following a storm. It is different in cities of the east or even in a city like New Orleans, where the detritus of centuries seems to nourish labyrinthine ambiguity.

Rocks and sunlight and sand are elementary and frequently dangerous. A landscape worthy of free men, they offer shattering clarity and silence."

JOSEPH RICE
Chairman, Irving 150th Committee

Owens
COUNTRY SAUSAGE, INC.
✖✖✖✖✖✖✖✖✖✖✖✖✖✖✖

There are lots of things to like about Texas but the
thing I like the best is the way people respond to a
remark about doing something in a new and different
way. The Texan usually says, "That's wonderful. I'll
help if you like and here's a suggestion that will get
you started." In other parts of the world the response
is, "It's never done that way and these are the reasons
it won't work."

Texas has always been fertile ground for a pioneer
spirit.

Jerry P. Owens
Chairman of the Board

P. O. BOX 249 · RICHARDSON, TEXAS 75080

crackers and homemade sausage and cheese from a small convenience store in Muenster; micro chips being processed where buffalo chips were once the order of the day in Lubbock

"I remember singing while at elementary school the words,

'Texas our Texas, All hail the mighty state, Texas our Texas, So wonderful, So great.'

Texan to me is not a state of being, but a state of mind. It takes hold and holds you fast forever. It is a good and proud feeling that cannot really be explained. It must be lived."

NORMAN L. MALONE
Mayor
City of La Porte

DOLPH BRISCOE, JR.
Box 389
UVALDE, TEXAS 78801

" As we look back on a relatively short 150 years of change in Texas, from a Frontier partially settled state, to now one of the great industrial and agricultural areas of the world, it is indeed challenging to imagine what the Texas of 150 years from now will be."

Dolph Briscoe, Jr.

CITY OF SAN ANTONIO

SAN ANTONIO, TEXAS 78285

HENRY G. CISNEROS
MAYOR

It began with _empresarios_ and a frontier. One hundred and fifty years later, we celebrate the Sesquicentennial--honoring the achievements of our history, but emphasizing that Texans today confront their own frontier.

It is a challenge that is as hazardous as anything faced by Stephen F. Austin, when he set out to build a city on 30,000 acres of virgin prairie in the 1820s.

Like any strategic planner in today's corporate boardrooms, Austin had formulated very clear goals. He had signed an agreement with the colonial government in Mexico City. He was formally named a land entrepreneur--an empresario--and he had to move more than 100 families to a new, uncertain future.

Austin is not only a capital in the governmental sense, but it also vies with Houston, the Dallas-Fort Worth Metroplex and an emerging biotechnology complex in San Antonio for the image of an R&D capital--the research and development that is so crucial to long-range prosperity in a rapidly shrinking world economy.

Pioneer Texas is now the Texas of major urban centers. We have become an urban people. More than 80 percent of our citizens reside in cities; less than 3 percent of Texans directly earn their living from farming and ranching.

This same population awoke recently to a new crisis. The price of oil plummeted to less than $15 per barrel. We have known about our need to diversify our economic base for some time. The issue of declining state oil revenues raises two questions:

--Has the leadership in each powerful Texas city put itself through a rigorous process of self-assessment?

--Do the citizens of our "engine" cities--the mainstays of our economy--understand their cities' goals? From the fast-food service business owner to the science teacher in the local elementary school classroom? From the corporate executive to the city council member who represents a large minority population?

If these answers are in the affirmative, then citizens in those cities will enjoy future prosperity. They will have asked the same tough questions that Stephen F. Austin asked before he forded rivers and cleared grazing land for crops. Only these questions will focus on what a city's population want their city to become in the year 2,000.

Texas cities in this Sesquicentennial year must be obsessed with results, where the leadership of the community--both civic and public-- know what their goals are and why they must be achieved, even if it takes the same sacrifice in hours, commitment and frustration that earlier Texas contributors made in the 1830s.

This is how I look at the Sesquicentennial. And this is why the city of San Antonio will close its year-long celebration of a proud Texas history with an event that symbolizes its future as a city.

On December 31, we will formally break ground for the Texas Science Museum--a facility that we hope will serve all Texas cultures, offer encouragement to visitors from throughout the state as a testimonial to past technology achievements, and finally, to keep our vision fixed on what is most important: our future.

Henry G. Cisneros

... a native son living in Belgium during the Sesquicentennial year whose longing for Texas was matched only by his craving for the state's official dish prepared by a master chili chef ...

ODE TO WICK FOWLER
FROM BELGIUM

By
James F. Widener

I'm nibblin' cheese and drinkin' wine
   and eating bread and jelly
Oh how I need to satisfy
   this longin' in my belly

It's Pâté this and Filet that
   and Belgian Chincorilli
I'd sell my precious soul again
   For a bowl of Texas Chili

Oh Lord, I see those chunks of meat
   a swimmin' in that stew
with plenty salt and lots of grease
   and onions, garlic, too

I smell cominos in the bowl
   where subtle spices dwell
And flavored like the Devil's breath
   with peppers straight from Hell

I know I'm comin' home in time
   and longin' seems right silly
'Til then I'd sell my soul again
   For a bowl of Texas Chili

... the smell of a water moccasin nest while water skiing on Cows Bayou; going to lunch with a Mexican-Texan friend in San Angelo and dining on homemade tamales

"Where else but Texas . . .

— does 'miles and miles and miles' have real meaning?

— is the 'Lost Pine Forest' not lost, but just a little out of place?

— is the mesquite too thick for a person or horse to walk through?

— can the jackrabbits outrun the pickup trucks, even in the wide open spaces?

— do the downtown skylines change almost weekly?

— do people say, "Y'all come back now!" and really mean it?

No place else but Texas."

STEVE BARTLETT
United States Congressman, Texas

State of Louisiana

EXECUTIVE DEPARTMENT

Baton Rouge

70804-9004

POST OFFICE BOX 94004
(504) 342-7015

EDWIN W. EDWARDS
GOVERNOR

On behalf of the people of Louisiana, I am pleased to extend best wishes to our neighbors to the East on your 150th anniversary as a state. We share in your excitement and pride as you celebrate your Sesquicentennial. "Laissez les bons temps rouler!" "Let the good times roll!"

Edwin Edwards

. . . . the paean of summer locusts at dusk; a steaming bowl of seafood gumbo heavily laced with crabmeat, shrimp and file from a roadside cafe in Bridge City

"Although I've lived in Texas for over half of my life, it was only when I went to Europe (especially to the Iron Curtain countries) when I really discovered Texas. From the people behind 'the Wall,' I learned that Texas is not just a geographical locale, but a way of life, a way of life where one can still dream of life's limitless potential — and still hope to attain it!"

LAURENCE F. McNAMEE
Writer and Educator

"Texas! A 150 year happening. The Sesquicentennial serves to remind us that our Texas Pioneers marshaled their strengths to secure a future based on determined self-reliance and rugged individualism. My! What an inheritance! Today, our contributions will serve to enhance that legacy for continued excitement and a strong future that's Texas."

GWYN CLARKSTON SHEA
Texas State Representative

LLOYD BENTSEN
TEXAS

COMMITTEES:
FINANCE
ENVIRONMENT AND PUBLIC WORKS
JOINT ECONOMIC
JOINT COMMITTEE ON TAXATION
SELECT COMMITTEE ON INTELLIGENCE

United States Senate
WASHINGTON, DC 20510

The year 1986 marks for Texas 150 years of proud accomplishments.

It was on March 2, 1836 that the people of Texas declared they were "assuming an independent attitude among the nations of the earth," giving birth to the Republic of Texas. That "independent attitude" has remained with Texas, republic and state, throughout the 150 years since, and has become a hallmark characteristic of all things Texan.

To the four corners of the earth, Texas has become legend. The blend of cultures from six governments, the heroic stand for independence at the Alamo, the colorful Texas Rangers, the cattle drives from massive ranches, the first gusher blowing in at Spindletop, the heroes and national leaders, the centers of learning and medical research, and the base of communications for the exploration of space -- all have created a larger-than-life image of Texas, a state where nothing is impossible.

Through the ebbs and flows of the past 150 years, Texas has steadily piled up accomplishments--a solid base from which to build an equally bright and inspiring future. It is with great enthusiasm and pride that I join all people of the Lone Star State in celebration of this Sesquicentennial year.

Lloyd Bentsen

eating a Fletcher's Corny Dog with a Belgium waffle for dessert in the shadow of "Big Tex" at the State Fair of Texas; a day's excursion and adventure on the Tex-Mex express train from Corpus Christi to Laredo

"The State of Texas certainly has a rich and beautiful heritage, and Texans have certainly made a tremendous contribution to this great country. When you think of Texas, you think of cowboys, oil fields, and vast expanses of ranch land, armadillos and horned frogs. We just want everyone to know that the Horned Frogs are alive and well, and they are no longer an endangered species in Fort Worth, Texas! Young men are now anxious to follow in the rich traditions established by such greats as Davey O'Brien, Sammy Baugh and Bob Lilly. And we can't wait to see the Horned Frogs dominate once again during the next one hundred and fifty year period. For a Texan, that's not called braggin', it's just called facin' the facts."

JIM WACKER
Head Football Coach
Texas Christian University

...cleaning an antique, engraved, nickel-plated, single-action Colt .45 with ivory grips and wondering what stories the gun would tell of the Waco policeman who carried it; a good feeling after dropping a five dollar bill in the Salvation Army kettle around Christmas time in Palestine

"Some people love the Texas weather. Some hate it. One man's hominy is another man's grits."

GARY HALTER
Mayor
City of College Station

"There are few states that have such a rich and well maintained cultural heritage as Texas. I am proud to be a Texan."

GIBSON D. (GIB) LEWIS
Speaker
Texas House of Representatives

"Increasingly, the world looks to Texas for originality and creativity in the arts. For so many years we have been importers rather than exporters of culture. I foresee an era of artistic innovation for Texas."

HARRY S. PARKER, III
Director
Dallas Museum of Art

...: a Sunday brunch complete with the nostalgia of ante bellum times in Jefferson; a psychokinesis seminar in Austin where individuals learn how to bend forks while nearby the state legislature ponders a budget already bent out of shape ...

"One of the cultural advantages of being a Texan is that you never have to apologize for being carnivorous.

Texas is just like the rest of the country — only more so.
I love the state of Texas: I consider that a harmless perversion on my part. Besides, I only discuss it with consenting adults.

What this country really needs, along with a change of government, is a stiff dose of Texas. Things still are the way they used to be down here and anyone who thinks that's quaint ought to come on down and look at it.

Texas is a dandy place, in short spells, for anyone suffering from nausee de Thruway Hot Shoppe. The state is naturally resistant to plastic, cleanliness and standardization. On the other hand, the reason it's resistant to such phenomena is because it's ignorant and cantankerous. Also, a lot of it is ugly.

The reason the sky is bigger here is because there aren't any trees.

The reasons folks here eat grits is because they got no taste.

Cowboys mostly smell bad and it is hot, oh God, it is hot.

On growing up female in Texas; I had a choice of role models — Ma Ferguson or the Kilgore Rangerettes."

MOLLY IVINS
Columnist

CITY OF DALLAS

A. Starke Taylor Jr.
Mayor

Perhaps more than any other Texas city, Dallas enjoys a
larger-than-life reputation...based on substantive success
and the popularity of the television series by the same
name. I do believe Dallas exemplifies the "best" of Texas'
indomitable spirit. On a vast expanse of prairie, people
made Dallas what it is today: the shining city of the
Sunbelt, a city ready for the opportunities ahead in Texas'
next 150 years.

Sincerely,

A. STARKE TAYLOR, JR.
Mayor

the mourning of a new generation of heroes and pioneers — Dick Scobee, Michael Smith, Judith Resnik, Christa McAuliffe, Ellison Onizuka, Ronald McNair and Gregory Jarvis; the year basketball fans realized that the Dallas Mavericks and Houston Rockets had come of age in the National Basketball Association

"Texans may have such a heightened sense of history because they have had such a definitive role in making history.

Hardin-Simmons University's locale in the Big Country builds in a frontier spirit. In many ways this part of Texas was the last American frontier, as the great historian Rupert Richardson has noted in his book, *The Commanche Barrier to South Plains Settlement.*"

JESSE C. FLETCHER
President
Hardin-Simmons University

...being carried aloft by mosquitoes while walking through Sea Rim Park near Gilchrist; feeling a sense of international pride in declaring that you are an American when crossing the border from a shopping excursion in Nuevo Laredo

"Texas is a special place. The history of Texas is a glorious story of success, triumph and accomplishment; of bravery, truth and commitment. And Texas has always represented what is best about America — freedom, opportunity, dedication, spirit and the will to win.

Texans are special people. They are honest, hard-working, loyal, and patriotic. When a Texan gives his word, you can chisel it in stone. When a Texan shakes your hand on a deal, you don't need anything else.

My success in the business world is due in large measure to the opportunity provided me by Texas. I know well what the 'spirit of Texas' is about. Here a man or woman with a dream, a lot of perseverance and a lot of hard work, can carve out a nitch, and be successful. Here in Texas we keep the American dream alive."

WILLIAM P. CLEMENTS, JR.
Former Governor
State of Texas

THE ATTORNEY GENERAL
OF TEXAS

JIM MATTOX
ATTORNEY GENERAL

Texas made the cowboy hat, the Alamo, and the oil well recognizable the world over.

But Texas also nurtured people who made a lasting contribution to the progress of social justice.

Texans were the cutting edge of the Farmer's Alliance and the People's Party.

Only Kansas passed an antitrust law before Texas and our statute was enacted a full year before the Sherman Antitrust Act passed Congress.

And Jimmy Allred sued Standard Oil and 16 other petroleum concerns in 1931 for violating the Texas law.

Jim Hogg's aggressive policing of powerful corporations, Sam Rayburn's political acumen rooted in democratic compassion, and Lyndon Johnson's ambitious social programs are trail markers for the Texas progressive tradition we should all take pride in.

Jim Mattox

...a Texas-styled 18-kt. gold watch with a pavé diamond face from Neiman-Marcus; a family enjoying the natural beauty of the Palo Duro Canyon while watching the production of "Texas"...

"Nacogdoches, the OLDEST TOWN IN TEXAS, is recognized as having the prettiest women and one of the best ten cities in the United States to live."

A. L. MANGHAM, JR.
Mayor
City of Nacogdoches

"Texas is my state. They fed me my first eight years in country music. They even played my country records on their pop stations. Like I said, Texas is mine."

LORETTA LYNN
Country Music Entertainer

... forgetting the educational benefits and sharing the joy and beauty of an exhibit at the Amon Carter Museum in Fort Worth with a young daughter; experiencing the cultural heritage of the Tonkawa Indians during a pow-wow on their tribal lands near Austin ...

"On the eve of World War II, the Texas novelist George Sessions Perry wrote a book called *Texas: A World In Itself.* His assessment of Texas' uniqueness may have been somewhat optimistic in 1942, but the years since the war have proved him right. Texas has, as the culture geographer D. W. Meinig argued, an imperial status among the states. Not only has Texas developed a unique culture, but it is exporting that culture to the rest of the nation and the world. Texas literature — both good and bad — is being read worldwide, and Texas movies have taken their place alongside those produced in Hollywood and other world movie capitals. If George Sessions Perry, who died in 1956, were alive today, he would be amazed to see how much Texas has really become 'a world in itself'."

JAMES W. LEE
Director
Center for Texas Studies

finding all the collectibles and antiques the pocketbook can stand at the First Monday market in Canton; a father's pride when buying his two-year old son his first pair of cowboy boots in Nocona

"As an Agriculturist, I'm proud of Agriculture, for it has developed the Great State of Texas. It has been a large part of the world's food basket. By Soil Conservation measures it is imperative that we preserve the fertility of our soil and take care of our water, native plants, and animals.

Then I would like to see Texas the cleanest state in the nation. That can be accomplished only by educating every citizen to handle solid waste properly. This we must do, else we will bury ourselves in our own litter and debris,"

GRACE W. CARTWRIGHT
Civic Leader and Noted Conservationist
Weatherford

...wines being produced with excellent character and body from vineyards near Lubbock; the last helicopter to leave an off-shore drilling rig as the season's first tropical storm builds to hurricane strength off of the coast of High Island...

"The State of Texas is quintessential America. Its population is an amalgam of the American people — immigrants from the other parts of the United States, from neighboring countries, from the other continents, mixed with Native Americans — and its culture preserves the best of each element.

It has been a colony, an independent republic, and finally a state within these United States. It was founded in revolution, fought in the War Between the States in what it believed was a just cause, accepted defeat without shame, and last sent its sons and daughters out to defend America.

Its people had the spirit of the frontier, were rugged individualists, men and women who would create a new world for and by themselves.

Its climate varies from the sub-tropic bayous to the arid plains. The world runs on its oil and gas. The world survives on its agricultural products and livestock. The world marvels at its technology that extends from far below the surface of the earth in mineral extractions to miles above in spacecraft, from microchips to better beef, from university laboratories to petrochemical plants.

One can be proud to be a Texan since Texas is the microcosm of America."

FRANK E. VANDIVER
President
Texas A&M University

STATE OF ARKANSAS
BILL CLINTON
GOVERNOR

I want join with all Arkansans in extending
congratulations and best wishes to our neighbors in
the State of Texas as you celebrate 150 years of
becoming a republic.

This is a very special year when both our states
are celebrating their Sesquicentennials and a new
awareness for our states' history is being
rekindled. I hope the State of Texas and the State
of Arkansas will use our strong roots as a building
block for a better and stronger future for our
people.

Again, best wishes for a wonderful Sesquicentennial
celebration.

Bill Clinton
Bill Clinton
Governor

Office of the Governor • State Capitol • Little Rock, Arkansas 72201

...enjoying fresh broiled Gulf red snapper Nueces at the Water Street Seafood Co. in Corpus Christi; wondering why the automobiles our northern brethren bring into the state have such difficulty in making complete stops at 4-way stop signs...

"I love Texas — and that's a lot of loving — it's so big."

PEARL BAILEY
Entertainer

"To Texans, independence is more than a state holiday; it is a state of mind."

W. MARVIN WATSON
President
Dallas Baptist University

ODE TO OKRA

By
John D. Vaughan

Gather the okra while you can,
While it is ripe for frying,
For this same plant that smiles today
Tomorrow may be dying.

Savor it now in soup or stew,
Or gumbo if you prefer,
And let its aroma fill the air
As you begin to stir.

Don't talk to me of kumquats
Or the rootabaga line,
For I have tasted okra,
And brother, it's divine.

I've sampled Albert Agnor's chile
And it has a certain zest,
I've dined on grits and hog jowls,
Corn pone and all the rest.

I've eaten gourmet dishes
The countryside around,
But a bowl of okra gumbo
Is the best I've ever found.

So gather okra while you can
And keep it on the table,
I'll come and dine with you, my friend,
As soon as I am able!

. . . a rush of adrenaline as warning sirens sound the approach of tornadic activity near Wichita Falls; a fireworks show and pop orchestra concert in Houston celebrating the nation's independence, the centennial of the Statue of Liberty and the Texas Sesquicentennial.

"I was nurtured, pushed, cajoled and encouraged by a hard working widowed mother. I was taught to work hard all during childhood and youth years in Oklahoma during the Great Depression. Our little family was in the 'proud poverty category.'

During those long drawn out years of higher education and military service, the most profound idea given me was from an accounting professor who did not fear the wrath of the Regents of the administration. He often stated during lectures that 'if you want to make a better living, you should move to Texas.'

I believed the professor and took his advice. Texas has been good to me and my family. Though never wealthy and retired now for some years, I love Texas and appreciate the good life our family has experienced.

I have valued the good words of that OU professor so long ago."

HOLLAND B. EVANS
Retired Educator

THE SECRETARY OF COMMERCE
Washington, D.C. 20230

The cowboy's maverick spirit and can-do attitude got started
with the adventurous men and women who dared to push West --
those whose prosperity came from the land and who were willing
to fight against great odds to win independence. It's fitting
that Texas is the only state that was once a separate republic.

Texans today can be very proud of this heritage, and proud, too,
that it was from the new lands lying north of the Rio Grande that
the strong, good and self-reliant Western breed took its place in
American life.

Malcolm Baldrige
Secretary of Commerce

. . . a small bedroom community being pulled into the twentieth century and sharply divided over the moral/personal considerations of a local wet/dry election; a child's constant hunger pangs because a family is too proud to enroll him in the school lunch program . . .

"If Texas were on Long Island Sound, and one hour from New York, I'd find it irresistible. As it stands, I find it almost that."

WILLIAM F. BUCKLEY, JR.
Author and Columnist

"Clint Eastwood says he has no higher political aspirations after being elected Mayor of Carmel, California. Just where else could he go for higher office — unless it would be Mayor of a Texas City."

JACK O. LEWIS
Mayor
City of Haltom City

"The difference between Texas and communist Russia is, in communist Russia the government uses the newspapers to tell lies, but in Texas we get to make up our own lies."

JOE BOB BRIGGS
Author, Columnist and
Movie Critic of Grapevine

...: the summer weekend bumper-to-bumper traffic on Interstate Highway 20 as horse race fans migrate to a sister state and enjoy a forbidden Texas pleasure; a father encouraging his son to cast his own shadow and to make his own prints in the sands of time while walking a beach near Surfside 🐾

"You're not a real Texan till you've been kicked out of every decent state in America."

JOE BOB BRIGGS
Author, Columnist and
Movie Critic of Grapevine

". . . my thoughts often go back through the years and across the miles to the freshness of that Texas air, the charm of all those Texas women (they were funny and generous), the blueness, greenness and sweetness of that Texas springtime, and the energy that suffuses everything in the state. Texas always seems new and young to me though it has a proud history. I felt then and feel now the State is simply bursting with good things."

HELEN GURLEY BROWN
Author and Columnist

listening to the ghostly echos of a Franciscan priests' Latin chants while walking through the Mission San Francisco de la Espada in San Antonio; strolling through the Lutcher Starke botanical gardens in Orange with youngsters who would rather be at Astroworld in Houston

"As an adopted Texan, the first thing I learned was that Texans really don't need to brag. The Lone Star State does not need to prove its contributions to the world hierarchy in government, business and philanthropy.

Just look at the names and deeds of some well-known and respected Texans: Ross Perot, L.B.J., Boone Pickens, Bill Clements, Dan Rather, and many, many more."

JOHN J. CASEY
Former Chairman and President
Braniff International

...: a lunch of fresh Gulf fried crabs, shrimp and oysters on the half shell from a Sabie Pass restaurant; creating a new vocabulary as oil prices plummet and "downsizing" now means increased company lay-offs ...

"One hundred fifty years ago 783 Texans, many of whom were not native Texans, under the leadership of General Sam Houston, won for us an independent Texas.

It is a heritage which they handed us with some giving their lives that we today may enjoy and commemorate these one hundred fifty years.

I was born in Weatherford, Texas sixty-six years later and today I owe those brave men a debt I can never repay. It gave me the opportunity to live in Texas where I have made my home the past eighty-four years with a chance to, in a small measure, try to repay that gift by serving my home town and community by rendering my efforts in making Weatherford a better place than I found it."

JOE B. WITHERSPOON
Potentate, Knights of Pythias
Weatherford

JOHN BRYANT
FIFTH DISTRICT
TEXAS

HOUSE OF REPRESENTATIVES
WASHINGTON, D. C. 20515

Texas. This year we are celebrating our 150th birthday--
the Sesquicentennial. However you pronounce it, it's a great
opportunity to celebrate the greatest state in the greatest nation
in the history of the world.

We have a history of independence here in Texas--a history
that includes the gallantry of the Alamo, the victory at San
Jacinto, national leaders like Rayburn and Johnson, the space
program, and much much more.

People around the world who have never heard of most
states know Texas. In New York, there's a Lone Star Cafe. In
Washington, D.C., there's a Texas State Society. Wherever there
are Texans, there is a little bit of Texas and a lot of pride.

Half a century ago, Dallas' Fair Park was the site of much
of the Texas Centennial celebration. We owe it to ourselves to
to make this year's observance a unique celebration, as we look
to an even more glorious, independent, and prosperous future.

John Bryant

. . .: a Saturday gathering of town locals in a cafe near the town square of Crockett to discuss and resolve all the world's problems and concerns; watching a doe and her yearling cross a dry river bed on opening morning of deer season near Uvalde

"Texas . . . a suburb of Heaven!"

> *JACK HARVARD*
> *Mayor*
> *City of Plano*

"In all my travels around the world, and meeting new people from all walks of life; my greatest joy is returning to my beloved Texas. The saying, 'home is where the heart is,' is so true."

> *DOUG SANDERS*
> *Doug Sanders Enterprises*
> *Houston*

... explaining the bidding process of a cattle auction to a young European boy at the Fort Worth stockyards; watching courageous pilots of the Confederate Air Force re-enact air battles of another period over the skies of Harlingen ...

"I propose a toast to Texas and the Texans who made her great.

Many of those Texans lost their lives in the Battle of the Alamo, but the loss of that battle only motivated Sam Houston and his 800-man army to work harder to make Texas a free republic. 'Trust in God and fear not' became their battle cry as they prepared for the Battle of San Jacinto. Surprisingly and fortunately, the battle lasted only 18 minutes and only six Texans were killed. The entire Mexican army was either captured or killed. San Jacinto was a decisive victory that changed the entire Spirit of Texas from near-despair to bright hope.

In closing, let me repeat some words of Sam Houston's spoken near the end of his public career:

> 'I made the State of Texas — but I did not make the people; and if they go wrong, the State still remains in all its beauty, with all its splendid and inviting prospects, with nothing on Earth to surpass it in its climate, soil and productions — all varied and delightful.
>
> It still remains the same beautiful Texas!'

Here's to Texas!"

CHRIS V. SEMOS
County Commissioner
Dallas County

...the recent past preserved for future generations at Old City Park in Dallas; a young boy chewing Days Work for the first time and realizing that in his dizzying state of nausea that manhood is not wrapped between a piece of cellophane

"The United States Navy and Marine Corps could not have won World War II as they did without Texas — without Fleet Admiral Chester Nimitz leading the Pacific Fleet, without Admiral Samuel Murray Robinson heading our massive ship-building program, and without thousands of fighting Texans like George Bush in the ranks of our sailors and Marines. If we ever have to go to war again, I sure want Texas on our side."

JOHN LEHMAN
Secretary of the Navy

COMMONWEALTH of VIRGINIA

Office of the Governor
Richmond 23219

Gerald L. Baliles
Governor

The Commonwealth of Virginia is pleased to acknowledge its contribution to the government of Texas. General Sam Houston, of Rockbridge County, Virginia, served once as President of Texas from 1836-38 and twice as Governor of Texas from 1841-44 and from 1859-61. I know that General Houston would be proud of Texas' achievements since his time!

Best wishes for a successful and enjoyable sesquicentennial celebration.

Governor

...young cowboys fostering a proud tradition by participating in the Texas High School Rodeo finals in Seguin; enjoying mesquite-smoked pork ribs from the Gas Station in Mansfield ...

"I'm retiring from the Texas Legislature having the same friends, principles and wife with which I entered. I consider that a notable achievement!"

CARLYLE SMITH
Former Texas State Representative

"I love Texas, it's just my size."

WILLARD SCOTT
NBC Weatherman

"It's been flooding again. Village Creek is out of her banks and the catfish are running through the brush, catching baby rabbits."

GORDON BAXTER
Writer and Columnist

... a family outing at Wet 'n Wild and discovering at day's end your body is cooked better than the hot dogs eaten at lunch; walking the decks of the Battle Ship Texas and listening to the voices of another generation of heroes ...

"Some things in life only occur once — one of those, for me, is to participate in the Texas Sesquicentennial. Although not a native Texan, I have lived here for over 25 years. During that period I have come to respect and love Texas more and more. Texas is more than a State — it is a way of life. The spirit of Texas is evident everywhere — in the U.S. government, the entertainment world, outer space, industry, and the field of education.

As Chairman of the Texas Society of Association Executives, I have had the unique opportunity of working with executives from all parts of the Texas professional and business world. It is indeed a pleasure I will never forget. Congratulations Texas and Texans, on this memorable occasion."

JOHN N. KEMP
Chairman
Texas Society of Association Executives

▲∴ ∵: a booklet prepared by each of Ms. Georges' elementary students which planted fresh seeds of Texas pride in a new generation of Texans; a small rural community where pick-up trucks coexist with BMW's, ranchers befriend filmakers and the tradition of the land is a fiber that binds each together ▲∴ ▲∴

"Texas is a place born of the bravery and vision of men 150 years ago. She, more than any other state in the union, has preserved her original vision for the future and appreciation of her rich heritage."

RON ADAIR
Graphic Artist
Designed the Sesquicentennial Stamp

medicating chigger bites after a day's fishing in a farm stock tank near Buffalo; the morning nudge of a policeman's shoe as a Houston street person begins to contemplate just another day on the streets he calls home

"Fifty years ago I had the pleasure of being the radio director for the Texas Centennial. I was also the author of the 'Cavalcade of Texas' which was the theme spectacle celebrating the 100th birthday of Texas. As a Californian who is also an honorary Texan, with deep regard for the State's heritage, I am happy to join with my fellow Texans in celebrating the 150th birthday and to remind everyone everywhere that while Texas has been magnificent under six flags, its greatest accomplishments have been under the flag of the United States of America."

ART LINKLETTER
Television Personality

Henry Ford II
Chairman
Finance Committee

Ford Motor Company
1205 Parklane Towers West
Dearborn, Michigan 48126

        "When the Lord made Texas -- and Texans -- he must
have been in an expansive mood. The land and its people occupy
a large part of American landscape and history. In more ways
than one, it is <u>great</u> country."

"Texas and New Mexico enjoy neighborly relations today, but 145 years ago we were at war.

The Kendall Expedition of 1841 still arouses debate between historical scholars of our two states, with Texans calling it a peaceful commercial venture and New Mexicans branding it a military attack.

During Texas' sesquicentennial, and New Mexico's diamond anniversary as a state, it would be appropriate to explore this little-known incident — perhaps by re-enacting it.

Most of what we know of the Kendall Expedition we know from the diaries of George Wilkins Kendall, a founder of the "New Orleans Picayune" who had come to Texas in 1840 to seek a new fortune. He soon found the financial situation was poor for the new republic, saddled with debts from its recent revolution against Mexico.

Mirabeau B. Lamar, the second president of the republic and the architect of its public education system, advocated foreign trade as a way out of the dilemma. Looking to the prosperous trade route between Independence, Missouri, and Santa Fe, New Mexico, he authorized William G. Cooke to organize a journey across the Llano Estacado.

This expedition will furnish an ample field for adventure. I am authorized to announce the names of Edward Burleson, Antonio Navarro, G. Van Ness and myself to represent our Government with the people of Santa Fe.'

Volunteers signed up quickly and on June 20, 1841, following a bon voyage speech by President Lamar, the group departed Austin bound for Santa Fe. Almost from the beginning, the expedition was tragic:

*On the first day, after settling up camp a few miles north of Austin, a prairie fire broke out when wind whipped sparks from the campfire.

*On the third day, one member, despondent over his own bad debts, committed suicide by shooting himself with his rifle.

*A week into the trip, cattle and horses began to be picked off by nomadic Kiowa and Commanche warriors.

*During the second week, several men disappeared, presumably killed by the Indian raiding parties.

*By the third week, potable water ran out. The rivers had simply dried up in the broad, arid plains of West Texas. Men began dying of thirst.

*By the fourth week, the expedition's leaders became disoriented and found themselves walking in circles for days. They began to discard their armaments and other heavy equipment. Disagreements broke out between the starving men over their course, and they chose to split up into two groups.

*Sometime during the fifth week, the two groups crossed the uncharted border between Texas and New Mexico — one north of the present-day town of Glenrio, New Mexico; the other near Clovis.

*During early September — more than six weeks into the journey — one of the groups encountered the first non-Indians they had seen since Austin — New Mexican shepherds tending their herds in the Canadian River valley. They were directed to the town of Anton Chico where for the first time in six weeks, they were able to buy food.

Kendall wrote at length of the hospitality he and his companions received in New Mexico, but it would be short-lived. Word of the Tejanos' arrival soon spread back to Governor Manuel Armijo in Santa Fe.

Armijo, loyal to Mexico and fearful of the Texans' intentions, dispatched troops to Anton Chico where both parties were located, surrounded and accused of trying to overthrow New Mexico. After negotiation, the Texans surrendered.

They were held at Anton Chico for a few weeks, and then ordered by Armijo to walk under armed guard to Mexico City — more than 1,000 miles away, down the Rio Grande valley, across the Jornado de Muerto and the Sonoran Desert. Many men died en route, but the bulk of the party reached the Mexican capital in early 1842 and were imprisoned there for up to a year. Eventually, most of the expedition's members found their way back to Texas or to the United States where their stories were printed in newspapers, precipitating the U.S.-Mexican war of 1845.

This story illustrates that relations between Texas and New Mexico were not always cordial and that Texans were not always welcomed in New Mexico.

I'm glad to see that things have changed, but urge both Texans and New Mexicans to find ways in which we can commemorate this historic clash between our two states. (2)

TONEY ANAYA
Governor
State of New Mexico

. . .: the year educational reform became serious business as the sesquicentennial of McGuffey's first reader was celebrated; rediscovering Guido's Restaurant and then walking the Galveston beach barefooted until dusk

"As the lone star in gourmet popping corn, I am honored to salute the Lone Star State in its Sesquicentennial year. As the largest state in the country, Texas is known world-wide for its bigness — of its land, ideas, dreams, or most importantly, the hearts and souls of its people. I tip my hat to you in this very special year."

ORVILLE REDENBACHER
Popcorn Expert

"I was born and raised in Texas. I've traveled all over the world. But Texas is always home. I don't think there is any place better than Texas. Once a Texan, always a Texan."

PAUL N. "RED" ADAIR
Red Adair Company
Fire and Blowout Specialist

176

JONATHAN W. ROGERS
MAYOR

"If El Paso were ever accepted as a part of Texas, the
State would be much better off."

Jonathan W. Rogers
Mayor
City of El Paso

. . .: buying fresh pink grapefruit from a small truck farmer in the valley near Edinburg; a group of Model A enthusiasts touring the countryside during the annual Azalea Trail Festival

"Texas is an entrepreneurial haven where you can grow greater, dream higher and accomplish more than any place on earth. Where else could a middle-aged grandmother retire, start her own business with $5,000 capital and nine friends, and grow to a $300,000,000 business in 20 years — only in Texas!"

MARY KAY ASH
Chairman
Mary Kay Cosmetics

"It's like my ol Pappy said, 'Son, always marry a Texas girl. No matter what happens, she's seen worse'."

GORDON BAXTER
Writer and Columnist

a newly-married couple walking hand-in-hand along the Paseo del Rio in San Antonio; a cool grape drink and a moment's rest while offspring ride the double loop roller coaster at Six Flags Over Texas in Arlington

"A born Texan has instilled in his system a mind-set of no retreat or surrender. Always going forward with never a hill too high to climb or a problem too difficult to overcome. In my political career, working with truly great Texans with those characteristics made every day of problem solving a most pleasurable experience. It added strength and vitality to every tick of the clock of history. I wish everyone world-over had the dominating spirit that motivates Texans."

BILL CLAYTON
Former Texas Speaker of the House

...wondering where some individuals have been all of their natural life, but being understanding of their having missed the best there is...

...a high school senior in Nederland giving his class ring to the love of his life and wondering if the ring will be lost before the love fades; buying ten pounds of fresh shrimp from a salty boat captain on the piers of Corpus Christi...

"Combine a vision of greatness with a 'can do' spirit and you've created an extremely powerful package. Wrap that up with a little bravado, and I think you have what is called 'the Texas mystique.' It's a positive approach to life filled with possibility and promise. Is it really any wonder people everywhere want to share in that gift?"

LINUS WRIGHT
General Superintendent
Dallas Independent School District

"I always say, 'You can tell a Texan ever time, you "cain't" tell him much, but you can tell 'em every time'."

TENNESSEE ERNIE FORD
Entertainer and Recipient of
the Presidential Medal of Freedom

Land is so much a part of the mystique of Texas. Our rich heritage is full of legendary figures who wanted to claim the land, fought to protect it, and were determined to make something great from the vast wilderness. They wisely used our land, in early days, to finance our government, to reward our veterans, and to lure others to come to Texas. Today our land continues to sustain us, and we share that same reverence for land felt by those early settlers.

Land--our richest legacy for all Texans for all times.

Garry Mauro

Garry Mauro
Commissioner
General Land Office

Stephen F. Austin Building
1700 North Congress Avenue
Austin, Texas 78701

wondering what William would say if he saw the replica of the Globe Theatre in Odessa; swimming in the Brazos River after completing a series of mid-term exams

"Today, that victorious day at San Jacinto and that first Independence Day are history, and freedom has been with us so long that we sometimes forget what it is. It is ironic that the man who has no freedom knows it best. But on this day we remind ourselves of the perils in which liberty forever stands.

And on March-the-second we pay homage to those rebels and rascals and renegades — those heroes — who in their time stripped freedom from a grasping hand — and with it won a justification for those who had died before and a piece of earth for their lives thereafter and for their graves and their grandchildren — and a homeland for us who on Texas soil now proudly and lovingly stand. We humbly give them our undying gratitude."

Dr. FRANCIS E. ABERNETHY
Secretary-Editor
Texas Folklore Society

JIMMY DEAN COMPANIES   1341 W. Mockingbird Lane, Suite 1100-E, Dallas, Texas 75247

Jimmy Dean
Chairman of the Board

Texas mystique is a difficult thing to explain
and I really feel if you cannot understand the
principle of being raised on pinto beans and
Bob Will's music - it is impossible to explain.
Texas is totally unique and I love it a lot!

Jimmy Dean

. . . a Texas-size steak with all the trimmings and tradition at The Cattleman's in Fort Worth; a year when gubernatorial politics degenerated from general mudslinging to contemporary name calling; a Sunday dinner table made more gracious with a bouquet of fresh Tyler roses

"San Francisco is both aware of and very proud of Texas' invaluable contributions to the progress, prosperity and well-being of our nation. Texans have added immeasurably to our quality of life — and we're very grateful for your efforts. Let's face it: Texas is big, bountiful and beautiful — and we certainly wish its citizens a very Happy Sesquicentennial."

DIANNE FEINSTEIN
Mayor
City of San Francisco

"Texas has brought a spirit of dynamic frontiership from the past to the present for the whole world to see. Freedom, achievement and courage are widely accepted characteristics of Texans. Long shall this spirit continue."

JOHN LEEDOM
Texas State Senator

♪ ♪: a Sesquicentennial celebration from January to December that united communities, showcased civic pride and rekindled a spirit noted in the old saying of "proud to be a Texan" ♪♪

Priddy Community Quail Fest: a quail hunt, arts and crafts, dance, hunter's breakfast, in *Priddy;* **Texas Arbor Day Tree Dedication:** a dedication of a pecan tree planted at the new high school, in *Smithville;* **Texas Confederate Heroes Day:** celebration honoring Sul Ross, in *Alpine;* **Miss Tyler County Pageant:** a pageant preliminary for Miss Texas and Miss America pageants, in *Woodville;* **Echo Jamboree:** country and western music in the authentic atmosphere of the old community, in *Echo;* **Exhibits of the Past:** a year-long exhibit of the history of *Sugar Land;* **Go Texan Days:** a chili barbecue cook-off, dance and contests at the fairground of *Navasota;* **Pancake Pig-Out;** annual pancake supper, in *Buchanan Dam;* **Sesquicentennial Ball:** a formal ball in honor of Miss Roma and her court, in *Roma;* **St. Joseph's Mardi Gras Presentation and Ball:** a Mardi Gras Ball with crowning of king and queen, in *Beeville;* **Black History Week:** a display of Black Texans in the city, county and state, in *Seguin;* **Pool trout Fish-Out;** a pool stocked with rainbow trout, in *College Station;* **Mr. and Mrs. Sesquicentennial:** a contest to determine Mr. and Mrs. Sesquicentennial, in *Athens;* **Jim Wells County Hoedown:** a big dance, rodeo, ethnic foods, and marachi, in *Alice;* **Soup and Bread Line and Sesquicentennial Style Show:** a luncheon and style show from the last 150 years in Texas, in *Round Rock;* **Texans By Choice Celebration:** combined celebration to commemorate Statehood Day and to recognize and honor those who are Texans-by-choice, in *Odessa;* **Amigo Celebration:** honoring an outstanding Mexican citizen who has dedicated much time and effort to better relations between the U.S. and Mexico, in *Brownsville;* **Fiesta Hidalgo:** a parade, carnival and dance, in *Hidalgo;* **Women of Texas:** historical pageant presented by the Houston County Extension Homemakers, in *Crockett;* **God's Carpet — Wild Flower Seminar;** educational program on Texas wild flowers, in *Yoakum;* **Bluebonnet Trail:** nature trips to see the flowers, and arts and crafts show, in *Marble Falls;* **Great Texas Quilt Round-Up:** an exhibit of 100 contemporary quilts with Texas themes, in *Austin;* **Honor Vietnam Veterans Day:** parade, ceremony and dedication paying tribute to Vietnam veterans, in *Premont;* **Old Zion Homecoming:** cemetery working by interested persons and former residents, in *Kennard;* **Tres Rios Bluegrass:** a weekend of Bluegrass music, in *Glen Rose;* **Schertz Senior Citizens Day:** the city rolls out the red carpet for senior citizens, in *Schertz;*

Poth Pirates Come Back: homecoming celebration and reunion at the high school, in *Poth;* Hamburger and Ice Cream Supper: a fund raiser for the Blanket Fire Department, in *Blanket;* Legend of Kisselpoo Re-enactment: Indian Princess Kisselpoo and her lover escape by canoe and the Moon Goddess retaliates, in *Port Arthur;* Shrimpfest: a celebration honoring the fishermen of Calhoun County with gumbo cook-off, in *Seadrift;* Big Thicket Celebration of Family Treasures and Relics; display of relics and keepsakes of the past, in *Kountze;* Polish Heritage Musical-Drama; the Polish heritage presentation, in *White Deer;* Golden Triangle Ski Club Water Festival: water sports and a ski show, in *Orange;* Houston-Jewish Texas Heritage and History: exhibit with special project by Jewish youth organization, in *Houston;* Old Time Camp Meeting: Brush Arbor preaching and singing, in *Saratoga;* Nixon Feather Fest: festival honoring local poultry industry, 5K run and bicycle grand prix, in *Nixon;* World Championship Barbeque Goat Cook-off: contestants from the entire nation, old-fashioned games, in *Brady;* Chili Superbowl: chili cook-off at the site of the world's largest bowl of chili, in *Buffalo Gap;* Tours of Clay County and Landmarks: bus tours of the county narrated, in *Henrietta;* Highland Hereford 150 Bull Sale: honoring Hereford's roll in the famous ranch country, in *Marfa;* Beef Syndicate Turkey Shoot: annual turkey shoot with prizes, in *San Isidro;* Flatonia Czhilispeil: annual celebration with a chili cook-off, in *Flatonia;* Buckskinners Historical Rendezvous Encampment; campout, old-fashioned style, in *Stinnett;* Terlingua Oktoberfest: a special Sesquicentennial German festival, in *Terlingua;* Red Bean Cook-Off: actual contest of cooking pinto beans, in *Palestine;* DeLeon Peach and Melon Festival: 72nd annual festival with exhibits, in *DeLeon;* Parker County Sheriff's Posse Frontier Days Rodeo; rodeo with horse show, in *Weatherford.* (3)

a year's celebration where the elderly remembered with pride and the young learned with enthusiasm

193

wondering where some individuals have been all of their natural life, but being understanding of their having missed the best there is

ART BUCHWALD

2000 PENNSYLVANIA AVENUE, N.W.
SUITE 3804
WASHINGTON, D.C. 20006

Dear Mr. Holbrook,

Forgive me, but I've never heard of Texas. Of course there are many places in the United States I have never heard of. I would like to contribute to your book, but since I am ignorant of what Texas is I better not.

Sincerely yours,

Art Buchwald

Art Buchwald

P.S.   The above is my quote, and get it right.

... recognizing in the final analysis that Texas is not an ordinary state, nor are Texans ordinary individuals; a 150-year legacy that is handed down to each new generation ensuring the spirit and heritage is preserved for those who follow us.

PHOTOGRAPHY CREDITS

*Photographers who provided pictures for this book are: Barry Snidow (BS), Jim Picquet (JP), Bob Amdall (BA), **The Journal** (TJ), E. W. Rock (ER), and Mark Holbrook (MH). Photographs are credited clockwise. Courtesy photographs are as noted.*

Page

6-7 *The J. O. Davis family, circa 1872 (JP).*

9 *The Texas Wagon Train. Courtesy of Triland International, Inc.*

10 *A real Texas wagon (BS).*

12 *Capitol doorway in Austin (JP); Old Fiddlers' Contest in Commerce (BS); Nueces oil derrick; The birthplace of the Republic in San Antonio (JP).*

14 *A yucca blooms in west Texas (BS).*

16 *Rio Grande flowing through the Big Bend (BS).*

19 *Old Mexican grave in west Texas (BS).*

21 *America's team. Courtesy of the Dallas Cowboys Football Organization.*

22 *Prickly pear cactus in south Texas (JP).*

23 *Big Bend vegetation (BS).*

24 *Big Bend vegetation (BS).*

26 *The Rio Grande flowing through west Texas (BS).*

28 *The blending of urban and homestead in Las Colinas (BA).*

30 *Fort Worth's famous watering hole (JP); Longbranch saloon near Coppell (BA); Ray Wylie and Bugs Henderson (BA).*

31 *Fresh from the Gulf (BS).*

32 *Be Bop Chili pod serves up a taste of hell. Courtesy of Mike Blood, Top 'O Texas Cafe.*

33 *Water from the wind (JP).*

34 *End of the day. Courtesy of Traders Village, Grand Prairie.*

35 *When does the parade end (BS); A legend continues (JP); Serious business (JP).*

37 *The bosun; After the ride; Continuing the tradition; Inexpensive Galveston hotel (JP).*

38 *The piney woods of east Texas (JP).*

41 *Big Bend grandeur (BS).*

42 *Party time at the South Fork Ranch (BA).*

44 *Wagon train bath facilities (BS).*

46 *Beware: horse kicks; Belton Skoal Rodeo; Replacing a horseshoe; Branding irons in the J. E. Connor Museum; A cattle chute (JP).*

48 *Fort Worth wildlife refuge (BA).*

51 *Sunrise serenity on Padre Island (JP).*

52-53 *The Texas Wagon Train. Courtesy of Triland International, Inc.*

54 *King Ranch chuck wagon wheel (JP).*

56 *Young pokes (BA).*

57 *Relaxing at Scarborough Fair (BS).*

59 *Remembering with pride (BA).*

60 *Lean boy; Mean woman (BA); The calvary takes a break (BS).*

62 *A new frontier (BA).*

64 *Rural entertainment; Marked for future reference; When oil prices fall; Rough earth; Seasons past in Round Rock; Hinges of tradition in the state capitol (JP).*

66 *RFD service, 1986 (JP).*

69 *Old Fiddlers' contest in Commerce (BS).*

70 *The Guadalupe River near New Braunfels (JP).*

73 *The Mustangs of Las Colinas (BA).*

75 *Mickey Gilley at Irving's annual TexFest (BA).*

76 *Corpus Christi shrimpers (JP).*

77 *A West welcome (JP).*

78 *Modern day bandito; Getting hitched with the Texas Wagon Train (BS).*

80 *A state of individual freedom (JP).*

81 *At the pool hall (BA).*

82 *Loading in the Fort Worth stockyards (JP).*

84 *Pasture pleasure (BS).*

86 *Georgia joins the wagon train (BS).*

87 *End of the trail (MH); Rough leather and rough ride; The wagon train heads west (JP).*

88 *The calvary rides again (BA).*

REFERENCES AND NOTES

1. McDonald, Archie P.; **Texas: All Hail the Mighty State;** Austin: Eakin Press, 1983. Permission to use by Eakin Publishing Company.

2. Loomis, Noel M.; **The Texas-Santa Fe Pioneers;** Oklahoma: University of Oklahoma Press, 1958. Source as provided by Governor Toney Anaya in his statement.

3. Texas 1986 Sesquicentennial Commission: **Texas: Official 1986 Sesquicentennial Guidebook;** Lynn Nabers, Executive Director, Texas Sesquicentennial Commission.